lissie

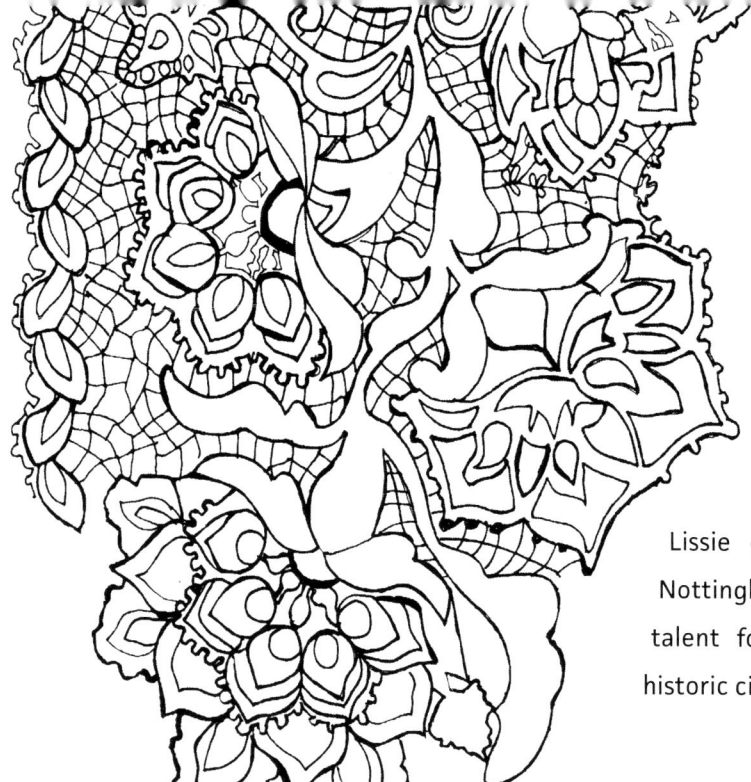

Lissie graduated from the University of Nottingham in 2016 and decided to turn her talent for drawing to commemorating the historic city of Nottingham.

with thanks to Alice for sprinkling her literary magic

HEY!

Happy Colouring!
Share your creativity at
@finelinesbylissie

Published by the Independent Publishing Agency

2016

Finelines by Lissie: Nottingham Colouring Book

ISBN Number: 978-1-78808-744-5

All Rights Reserved
© Copyright 2017

Printed by BookPrintingUK

Script Edited by Alice Bell

Illustrations by Alicia Hollis

Lissie Art ©

www.lissieart.com/finelines

NOTTINGHAM
-
OLD MARKET SQUARE
-
THE UNIVERSITY OF NOTTINGHAM
-
WOLLATON HALL AND PARK
-
NOTTINGHAM TRENT UNIVERSITY
-
CASTLE AND CAVES
-
ROBIN HOOD
-
GREEN'S WINDMILL
-
GOOSE FAIR
-
SHERWOOD FOREST
-
AY UP ME DUCK
-
NOTTINGHAM CONTEMPORARY
-
CASTLE WARF AND CANAL
-
THE LACE MARKET
-
NEWSTEAD ABBEY
-
TRENT BRIDGE
-
THE DUKE OF NEWCASTLE'S TUNNEL
-
THE ARBORETUM
-
YE OLDE TRIP TO JERUSALEM
-
VICTORIA MEMORIAL

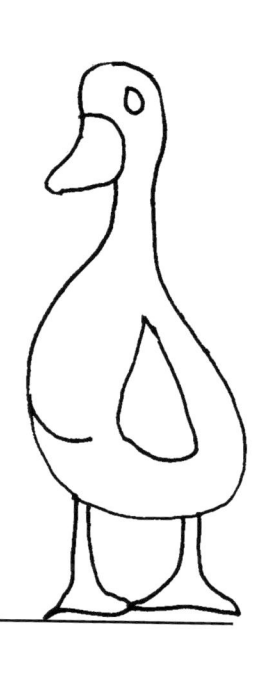

1

> Share your colouring! tag @finelinesbylissie to show the community

Nottingham

- Nottingham

Nothing sums up the endearing nature of Nottingham better than the local greeting 'Ay up duck'; friendly, cheery, and oddly pastoral all at once. Nottingham is probably most famous world wide for its connection to the 13th Century folk hero, Robin Hood, and more recently for its illustrious history in Lace manufacture. Nowadays Nottingham is known for its vibrant music scene, independent businesses and diverse culture. Its closest neighbouring cities are Derby, Leicester and Lincoln and is around 50 miles away from the capital of the Midlands and England's second largest city: Birmingham.

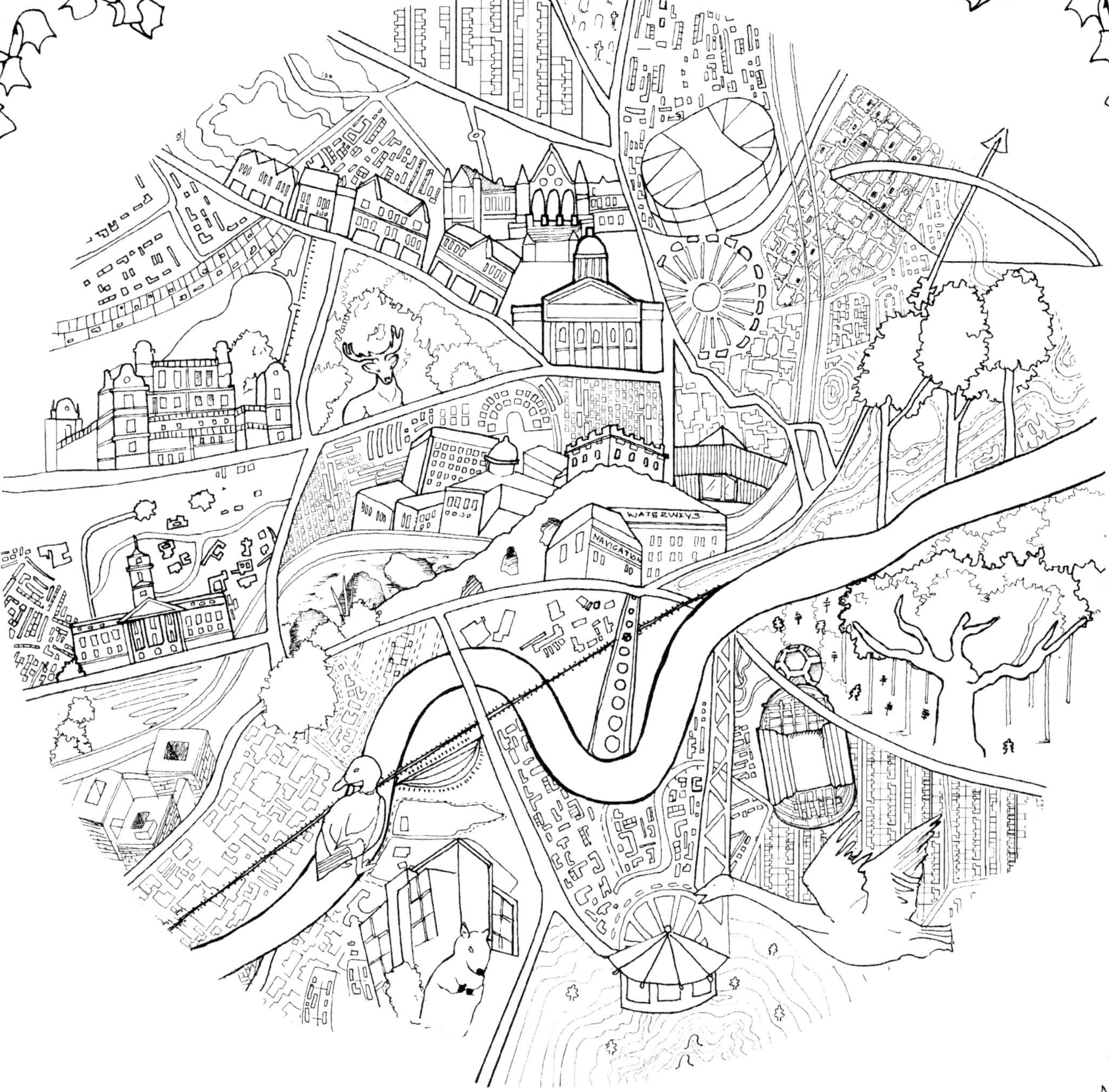
WATERWAYS
NAVIGATION

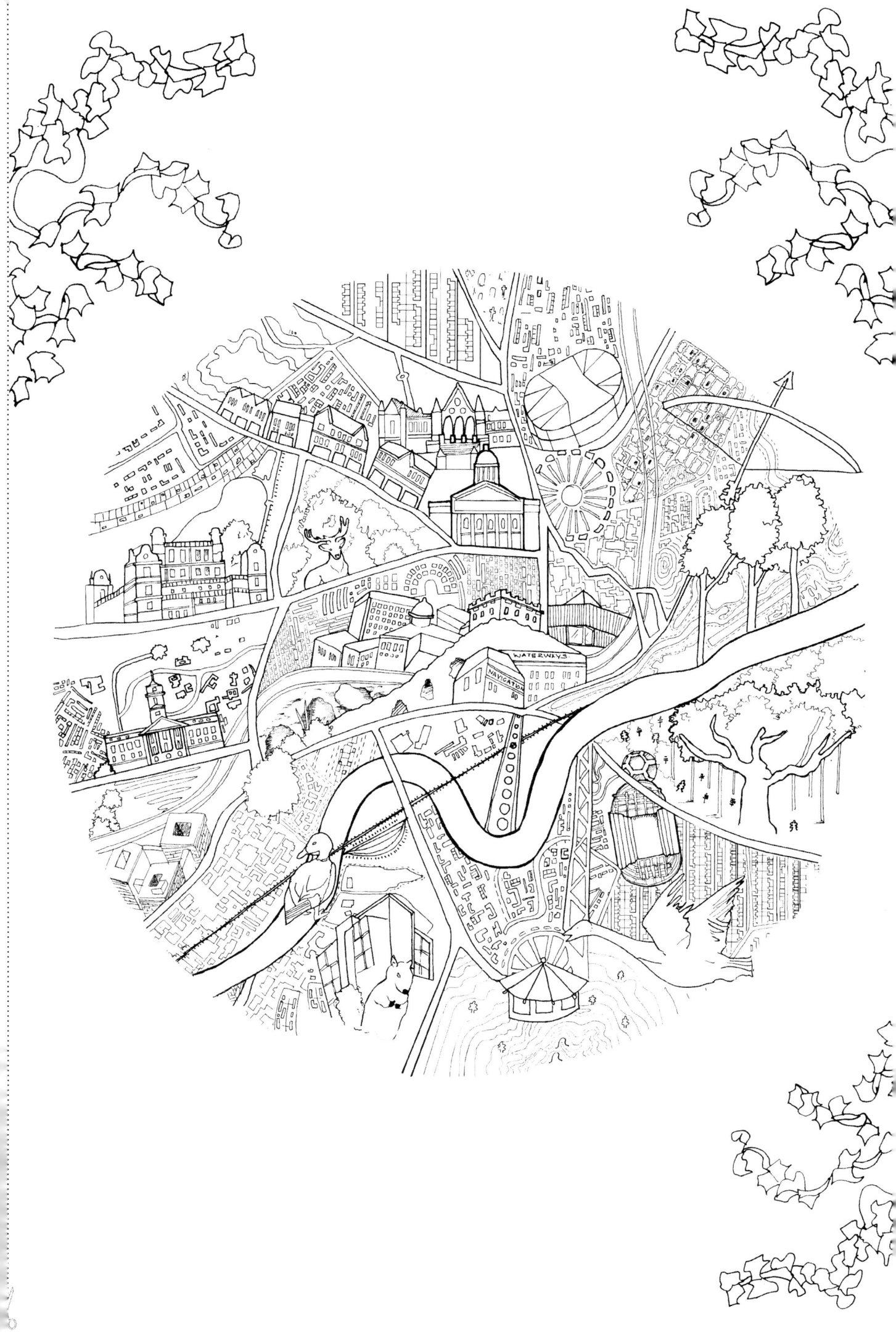

2

OLD MARKET SQUARE

The Old Market Square is a beautiful, fully pedestrian area of Nottingham City centre which sits in the shadow of the Council House and Nottingham's City Hall.

This square is the heart of the city, hosting everything from the German Christmas Market in winter, year round events featuring local food and crafts, and has been the backdrop to less commercial events, such as protests.

Over 700 years ago, it was the original setting for the Nottingham Goose Fair which, as the city grew, was moved to Forest Recreation ground. One of the more memorable symbols of Nottingham is the twinned lions guarding the Council House. The pair, in some circles, are known as Lennie and Ronnie.

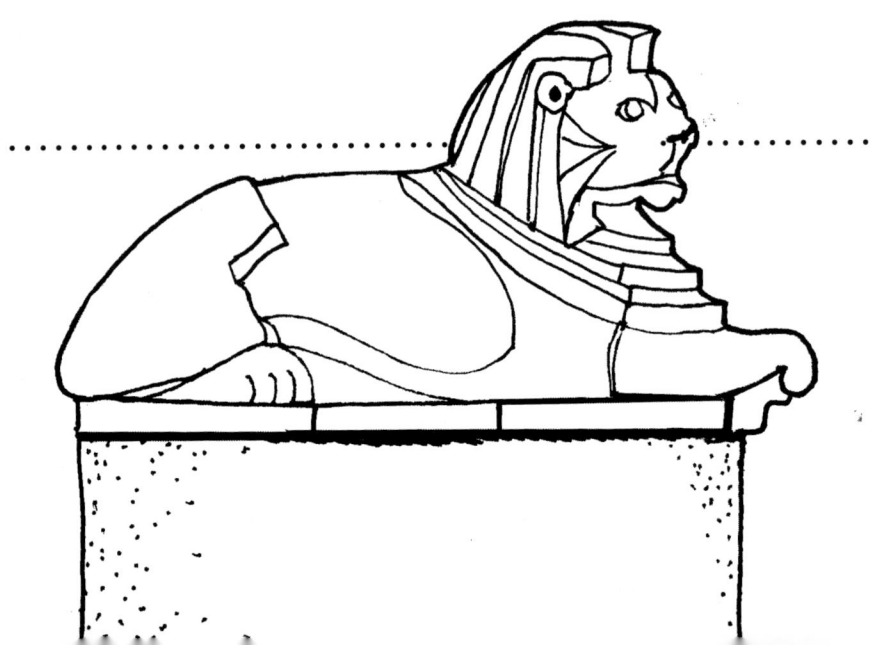

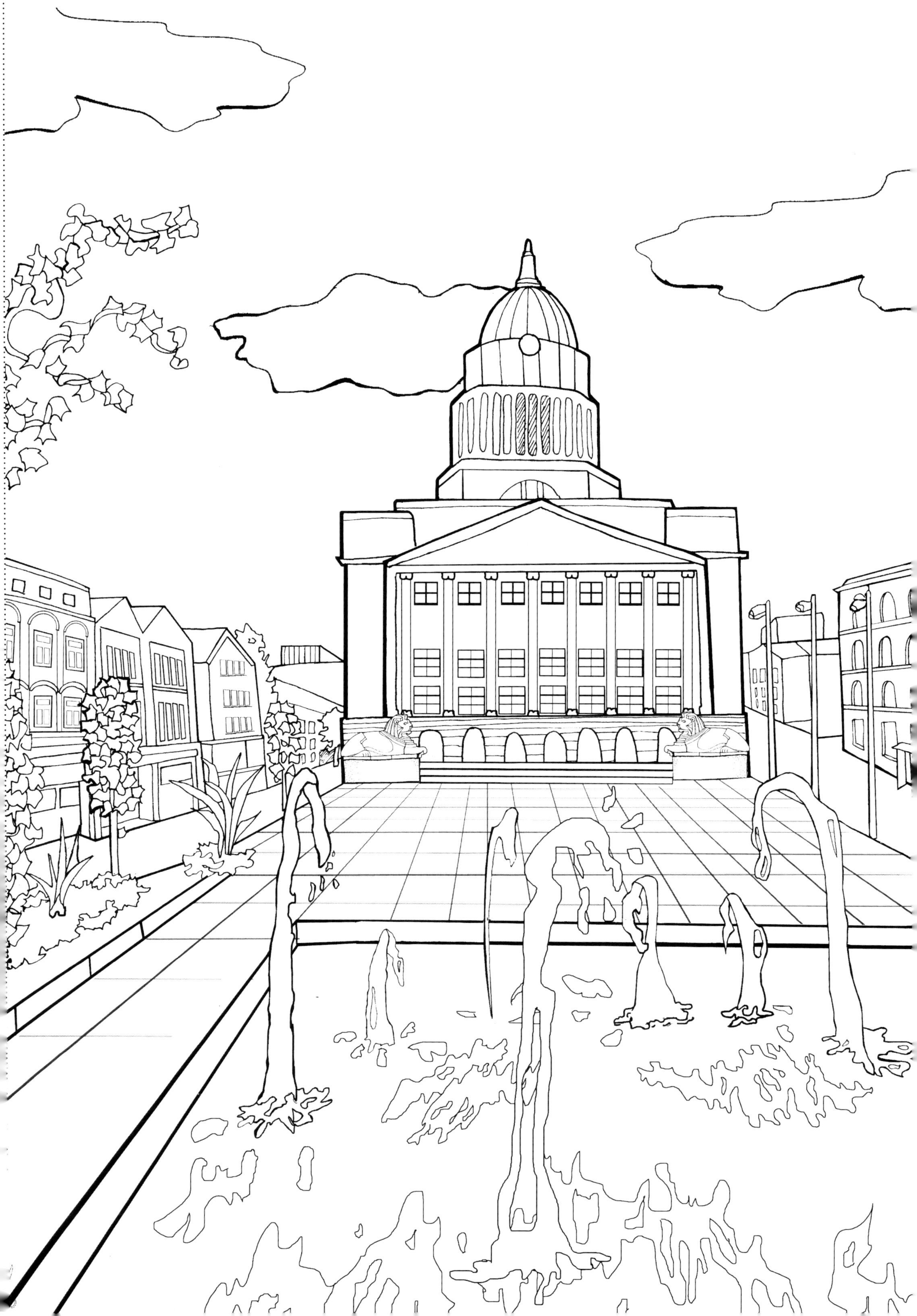

3

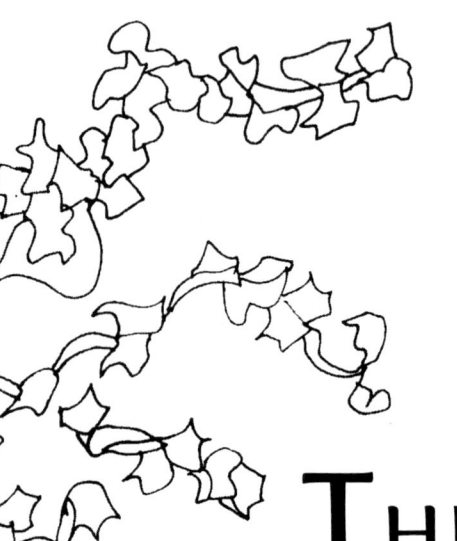

The University of Nottingham

The University of Nottingham can trace its origins to an adult education centre established in 1798. Over the early 20th Century the campus was moved to Highfields Park after a generous land donation from Lord Trent. The campus is to the west of the city centre, with the beautiful greenery acting as an oasis that makes it easy to forget that you are still next to one of the main roads in and out of the city. The iconic image of the University is of the grandiose Trent building rising above the tranquil lake of Highfields park; more recently this image has shifted to include the two lions that echo those in the city centre, a gift from Nottingham's international campuses. On any given day you can find students, lecturers, and locals alike strolling about campus, and occasionally the geese who like to cause a minor traffic jam, crossing from one green space to another.

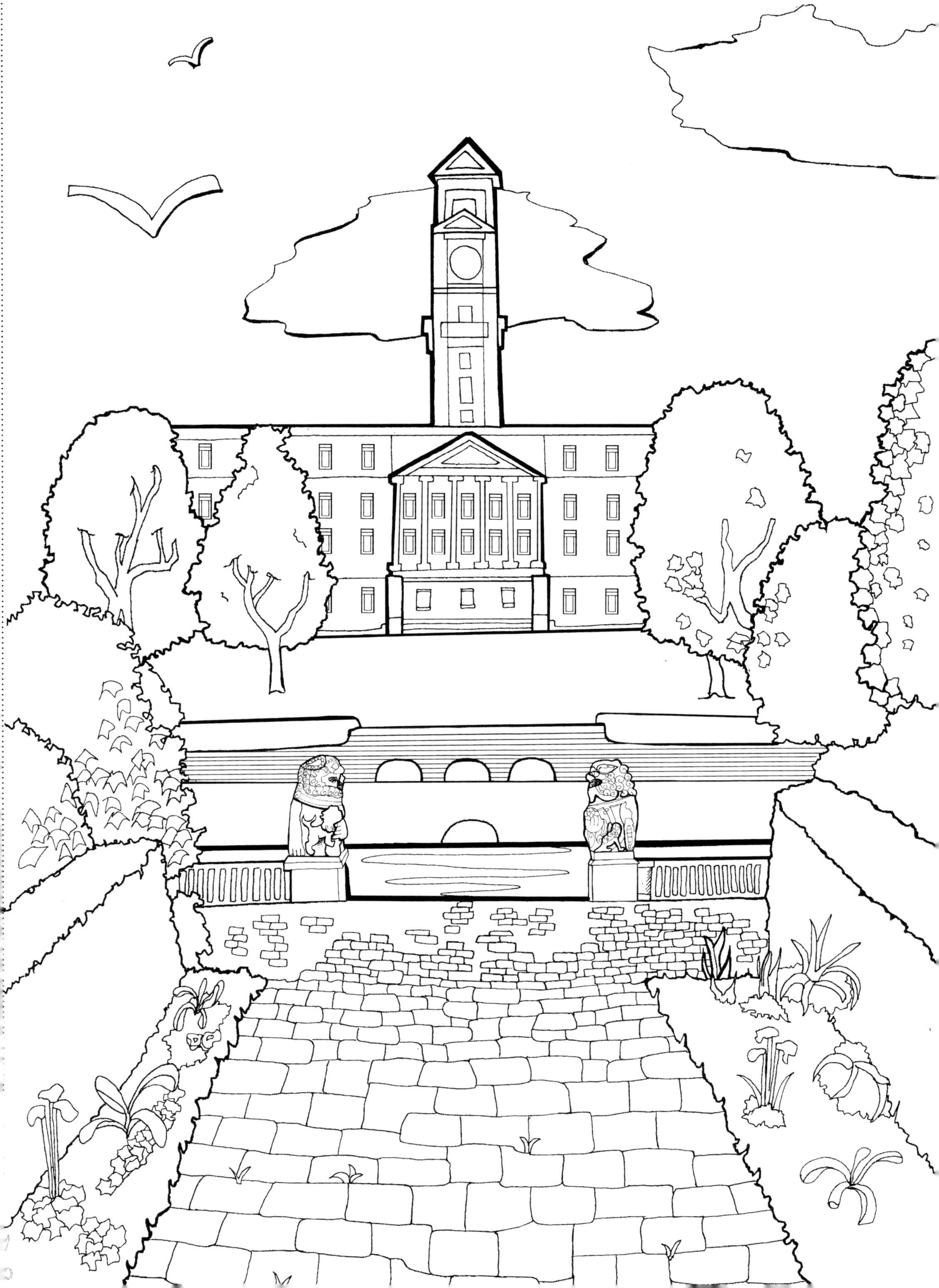

PSST! *There's a secret club... go to **page 44** ...but don't tell anyone!*

WOLLATON HALL AND PARK

Wollaton Park is surprisingly peaceful given its location just off of some of the busiest roads to and from the city, the ideal location for a peaceful walk all year round.

The Manor, built in the 1580s, was occupied by the Willoughby family until 1925, when it was bought by the Nottingham City Council. Under Nottingham City Museums and Galleries it has become a home to an astounding collection of galleries, from world-spanning Natural History to the more localised history of the house.

In recent popular culture Wollaton Hall has been home to the hero Nottingham needs, Batman. Much of Christopher Nolan's - *The Dark Knight Rises* - was filmed in the UK, and Wollaton Hall became the exterior location for the reconstructed Wayne Manor. Coincidentally or not, there is a village not too far out from the main city called Gotham - thankfully, not as riddled with crime as its fictional counterpart.

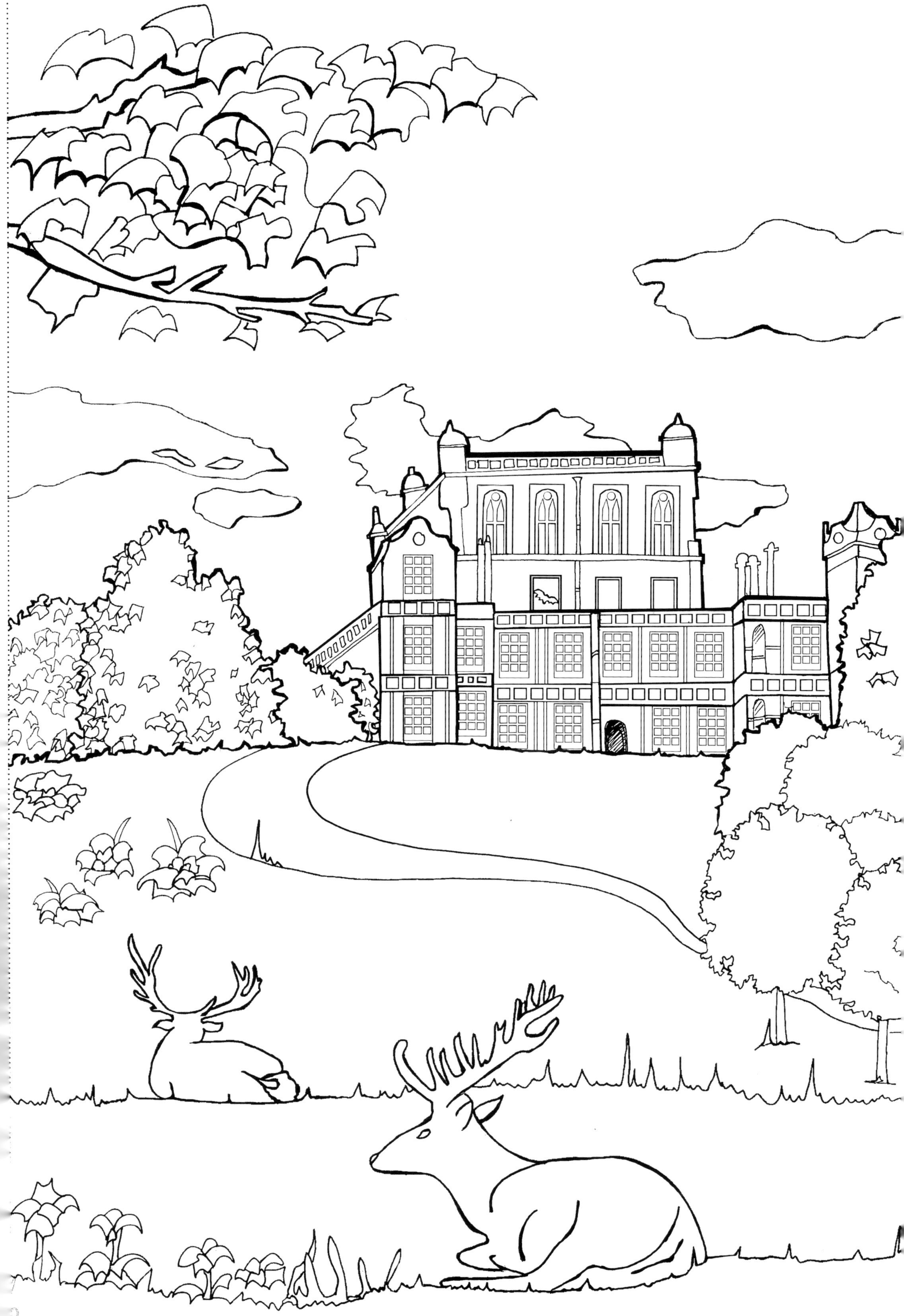

5
Nottingham Trent University

Nottingham Trent University has some of the highest regarded Art and Design courses in the country, due in no small part to its origins as the Nottingham Government School of Design in 1843. Becoming a University in 1992 it is situated in the heart of city life, unlike their campus oriented cousins across the other side of the city. This puts its students in a perfect position to enjoy Nottingham's incredible nightlife, including their own Student Union bar. Possibly the most famous building related to Nottingham Trent is the Artwright Building, a Grade II listed building that stands beautifully stark against the more modern architecture of the more recent university buildings. Trent and UoN have a fierce, only somewhat serious, rivallry, with the healthiest and most famous outlet for this being exercised in the Varsity series, the highlight of both Universities' calendars.

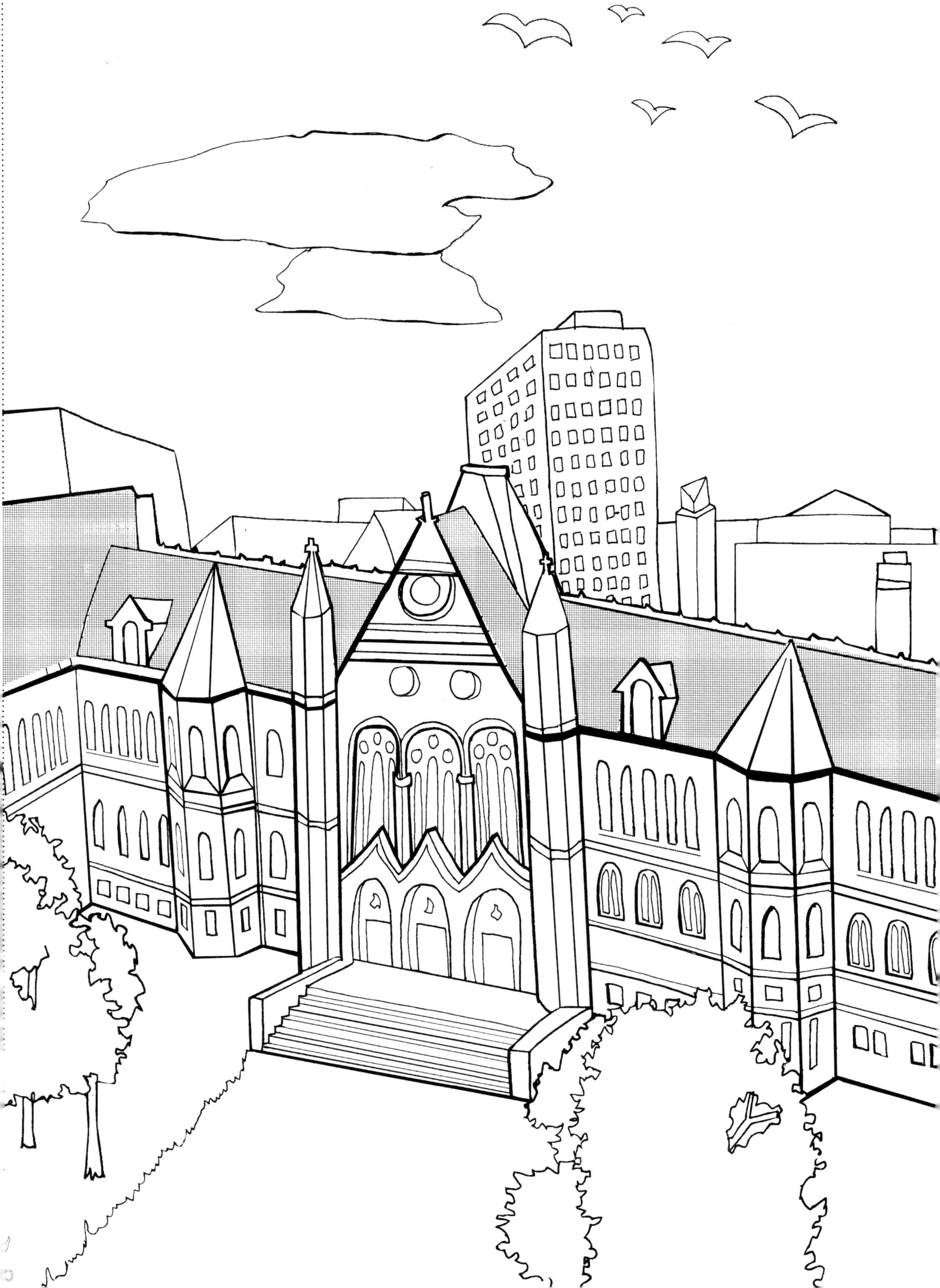

6

Nottingham Castle and Caves
+ THE MUSEUM OF NOTTINGHAM LIFE

Nottingham Castle stands proud at the top of Castle Rock, making it the grandest yet most unusual sites near the city centre. Damage by the royalists in the English Civil War means that little of the original castle remains.

In the centuries prior to its destruction the noble classes would call the castle their home from home, with easy access to the River Trent and plenty of game to be hunted in nearby Sherwood Forest. A mansion was built to replace the castle palace, which didn't last all that long either. Its destructive end came in 1831 when rioters set it alight.

Today the site is open to the public with a rotating series of art collections, history exhibitions and archaeological studies that explore the local area.

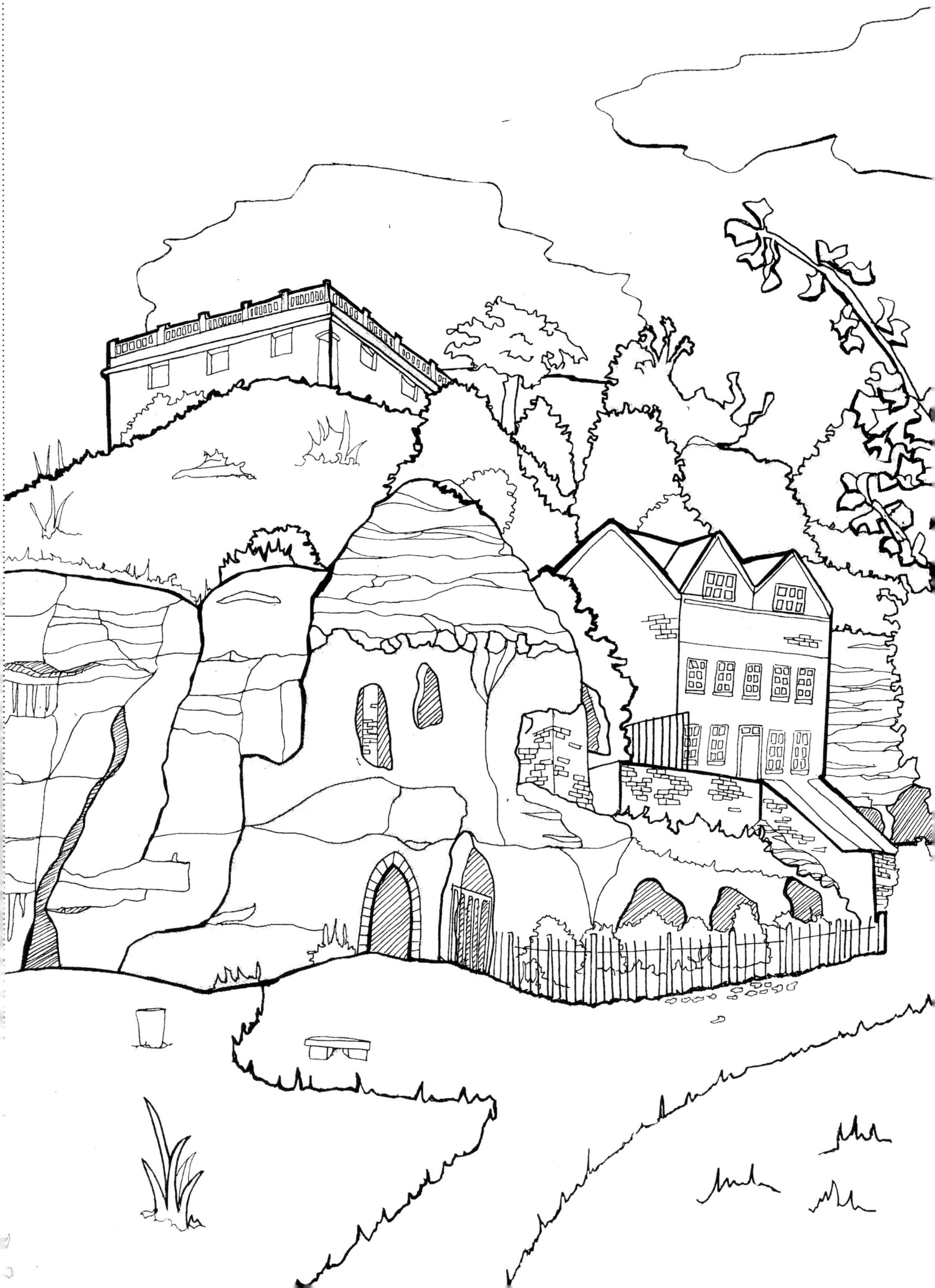

7

ROBIN HOOD

One of Nottingham's most famous exports has to be Robin Hood, although if there ever was a real figure who stole from the rich to give to the poor is a matter up for intense debate. The dashing outlaw and his band of merry men have helped to place Nottingham on the world stage, with their tales being adapted for TV and Cinema over 68 times, and the image of a band of jolly outlaws has been the basis of countless other characters.

According to legend, he lived in Sherwood Forest, hiding from his cruel and greedy rival, the Sheriff of Nottingham. It is due to his influence that Nottingham is so strongly associated with the colour green, given the multiple early depictions of the thief in rich green clothing. Interestingly, this shade is named 'Lincoln Green' for the dyers of Lincoln, who were able to create such a distinctive and unique shade.

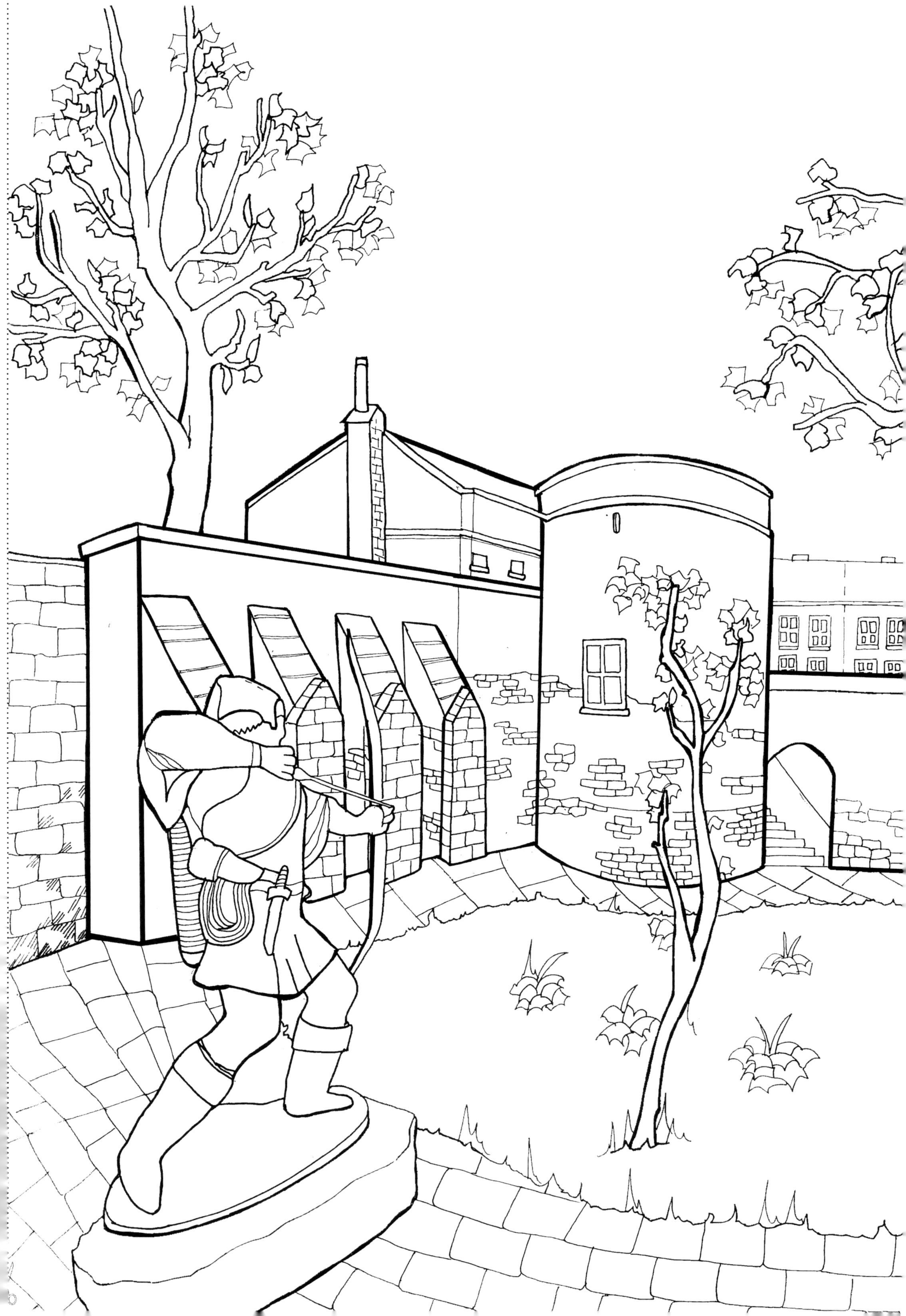

8
Green's Windmill

Nottingham is hardly the first place you would associate with the pastoral image of a gently turning windmill, but this city is full of surprises when you go off the beaten track. Green's Windmill is a fully functional 19th century tower windmill in Sneinton that was built in 1807 by the hugely influential mathematical physicist George Green, and was used as a mill until the 1860s. After centuries of disrepair Nottingham City Council acquired the Grade II listed building and funded it's renovation and conversion into a scientific centre, in honour of the famous scientist who initially built it. True to Green's work on magnetism and electricity, visitors can participate in their own rudimentary experiments with physics. One of the greatest things about this attraction? It's completely free!

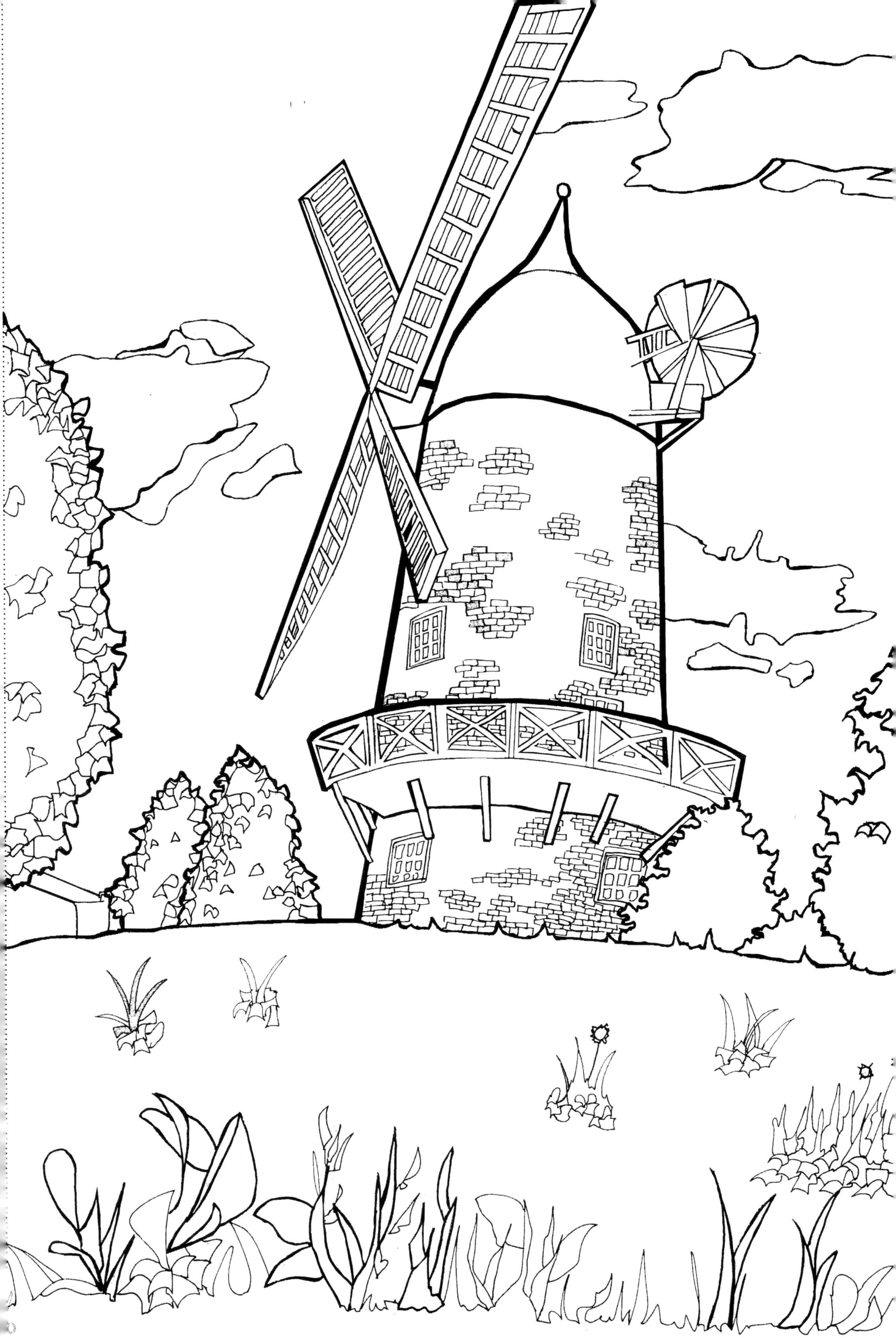

9
Forest Recreational Ground +Goose Fair

A quick tram ride from the city centre is the Forest Recreation Ground. It is the site for the annual Goose Fair in October, originally held in Old Market Square, and houses several interesting historical attractions such as the original Grade II listed Police Lodge- named Forest Lodge - built in 1857. The cell can still be seen inside, but it is no longer used to detain the miscreants of Nottingham. Today you can expect to find the vast open space used for sports for all the community, as has been done for the past three centuries. The local football team, Nottingham Forest used to play on the ground and may well owe their name, if not their league position to Forest Rec'. Another popular event is the Bonfire Night display, a draw for all the family.

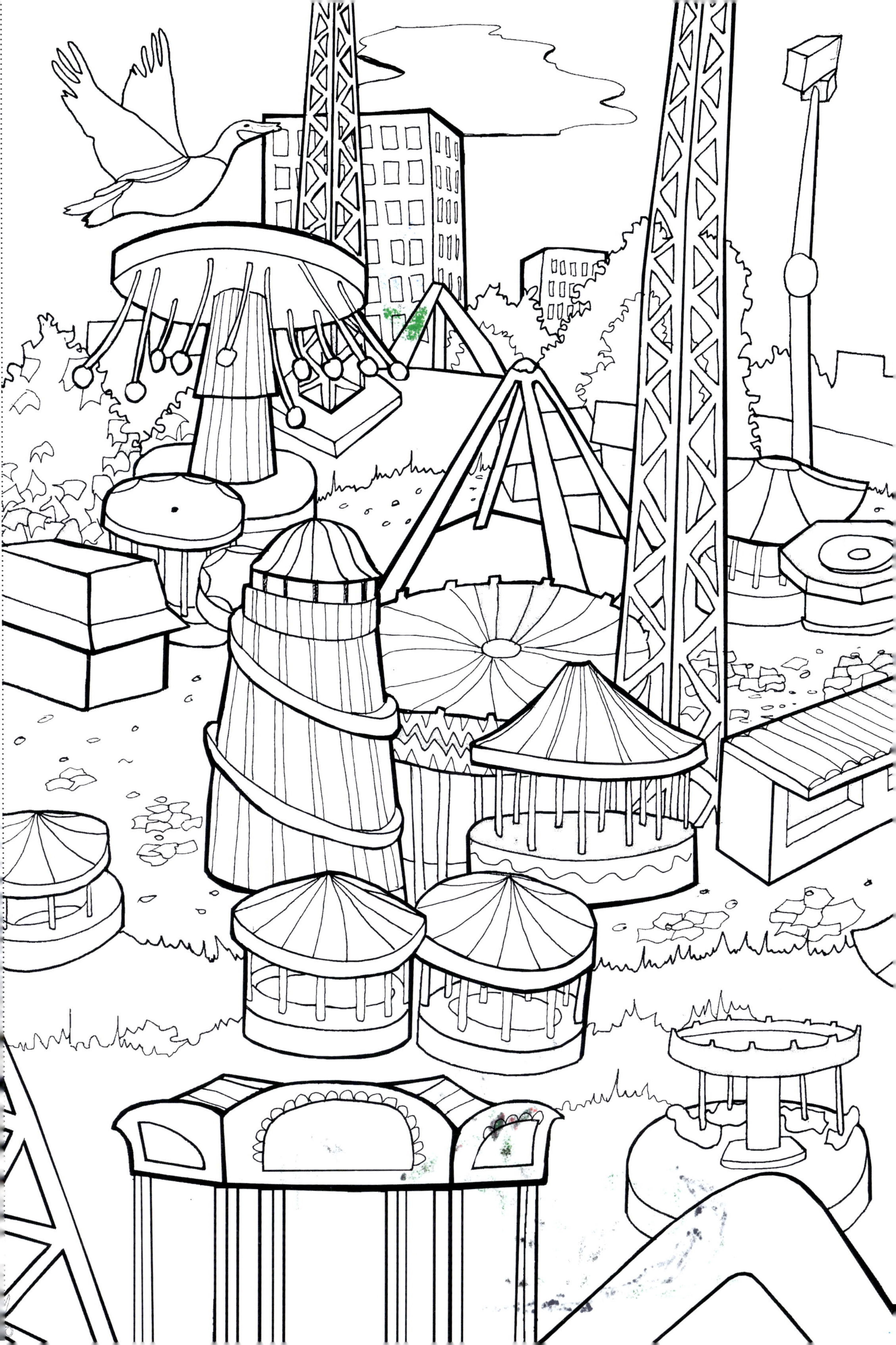

10

SHERWOOD FOREST

Robin Hood's old stomping ground and setting for his many adventures, Sherwood Forest is probably one of the most famous forests in the world due to its association with the legendary outlaw. Within the 400 hectares of National Nature Reserve is one very famous tree: the Major Oak, an ancient bush that is so sprawling that maintaining it requires lots of extra support. Thankfully Victorians built a ingenuous support system, ensuring its survival so that it could be featured on the BBC program Seven Natural Wonders.

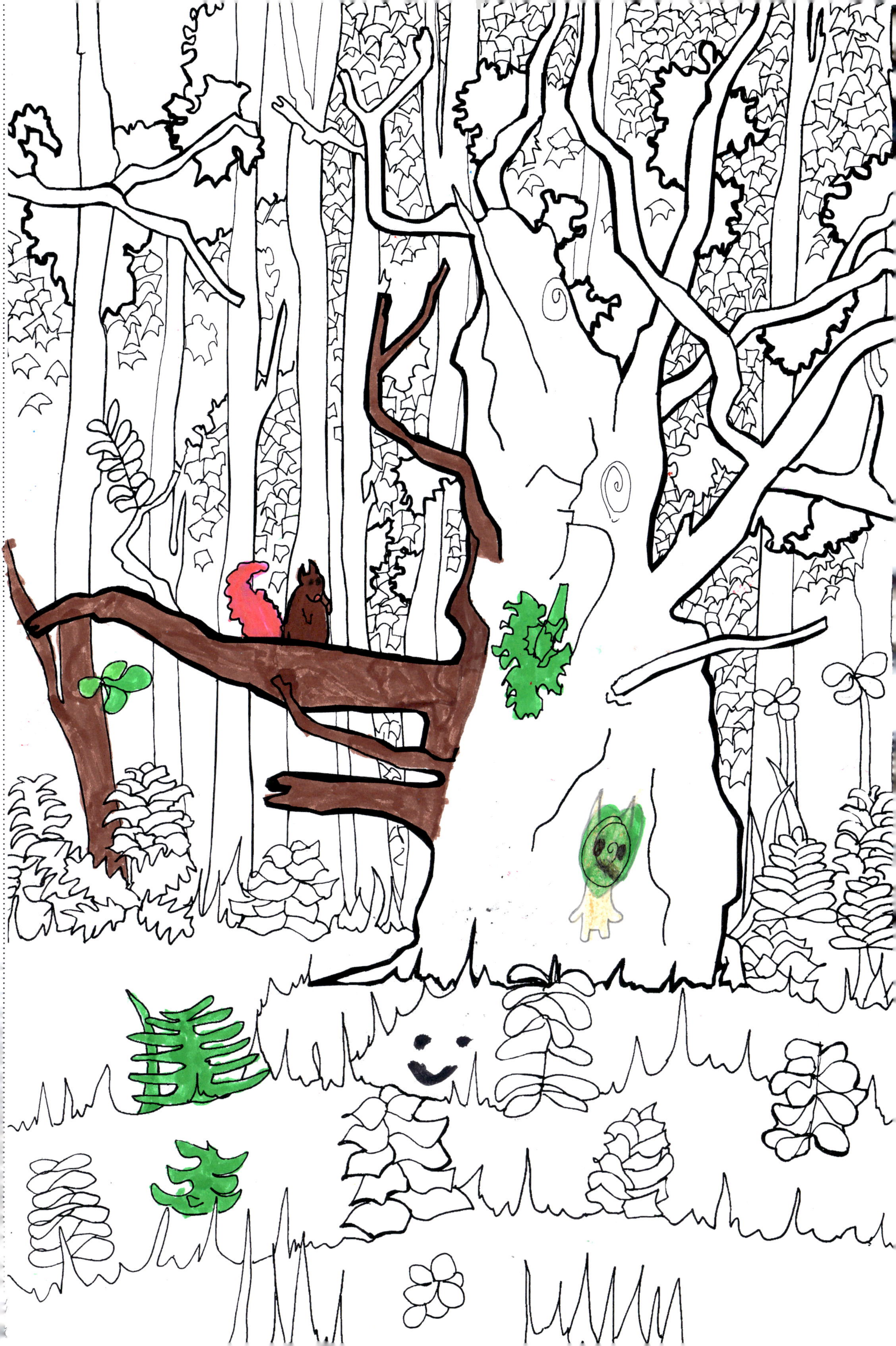

11

Ay Up Me Duck

The familiar and friendly greeting has been used for years across the Midlands, where you are likely to be called Duck, ducky or Mi-duck. The endearing phrase is gender neutral with both men and women using it to address just about anyone in the area. It is theoried that 'Ay up' originates from the Old Norse for 'watch out' and that Duck may have travelled down from addressing someone as Duke, and probably had nothing to do with the feathered bird we know today. The multi-award winning actress, Angelina Jolie, famously used the phrase when presenting an award to co-actor Jack O'Connel, who is from the East Midlands.

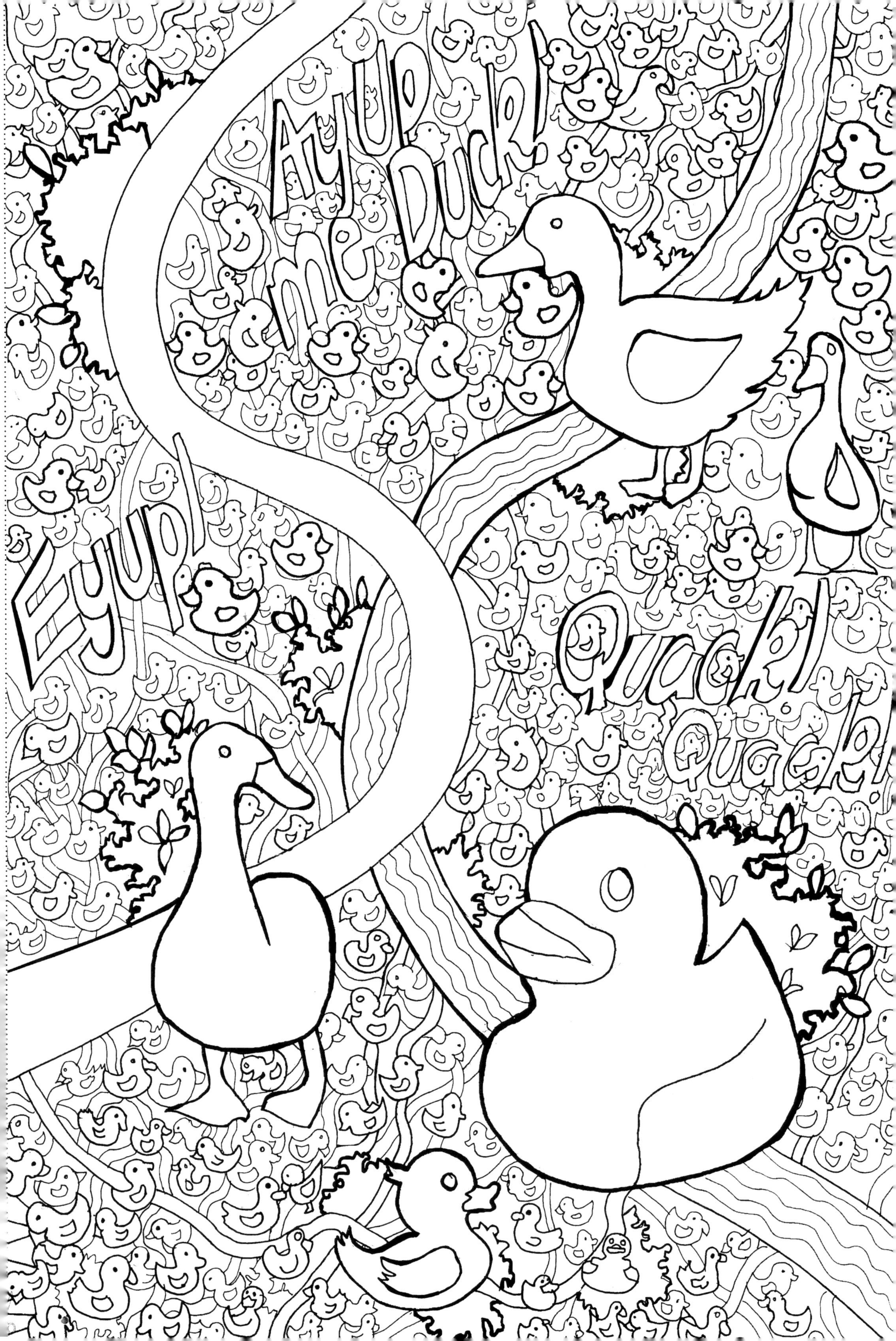

Ay Up me Duck!
Eyup!
Quack!
Quack!

12
Nottingham Contemporary

The two most noteworthy sites in this otherwise urban setting are Nottingham Contemporary and Pitcher and Piano, a little bit of picturesque history towards the outskirts of the main city. Pitcher and Piano was converted from a church dating back to 1690, now it is a stunning mix of modern and traditional design, the perfect place to grab a drink and relax.

The Nottingham Contemporary is a modern art museum, open to all and completely free. On any given day you can find an incredible array of cultural exhibitions and there are numerous special events for the whole family. Designed by award winning architects, Caruso St John, each element was carefully considered; the floor to ceiling window that frames the Church Spire, to the 132 skylights that illuminate the exhibitions.

HEY!

Love those colours!

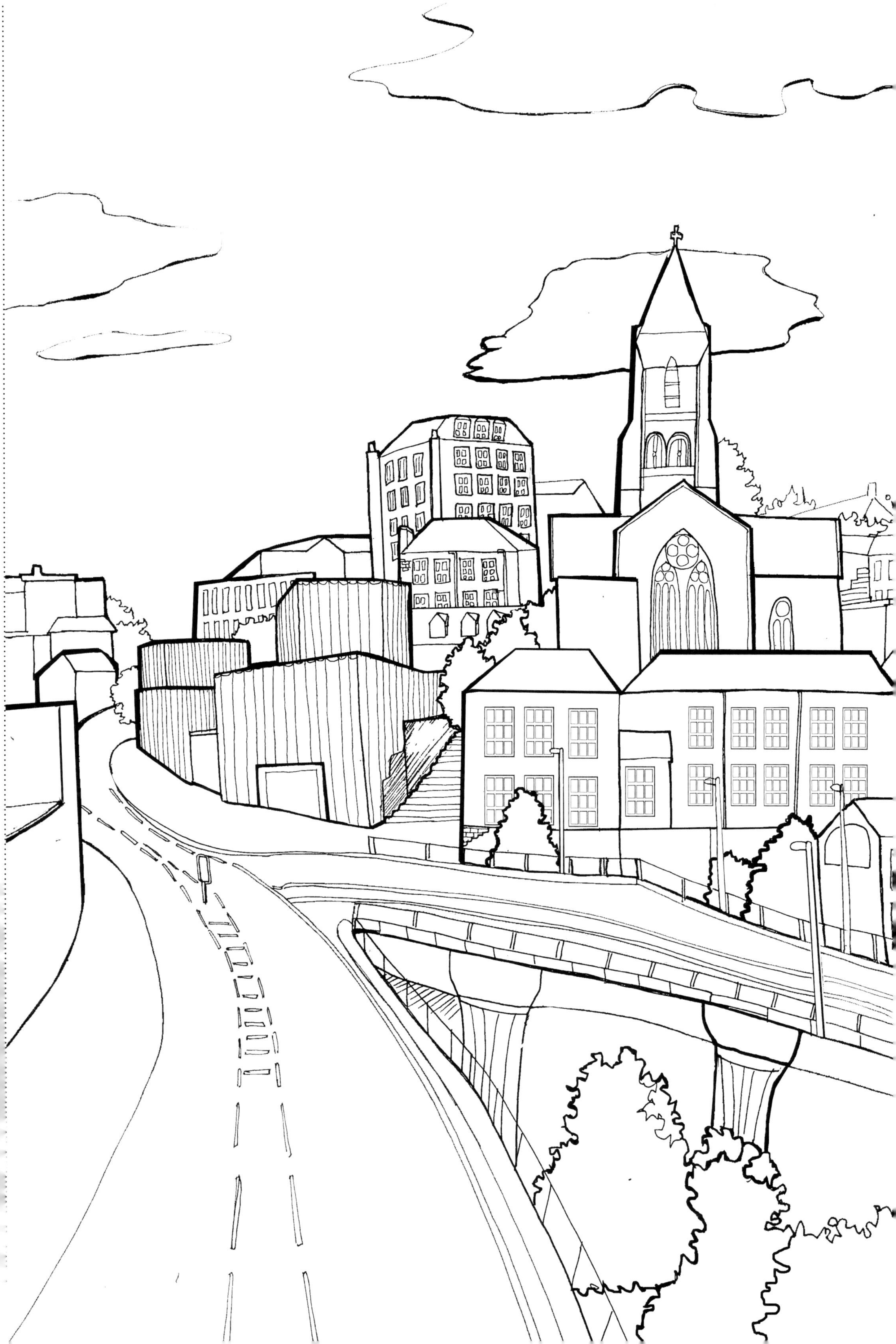

13

CASTLE WARF AND CANAL

Prior to the lorries and cars that are used today, the chief mode of transport were horses and canals. Nottingham canal was constructed in 1792 to transport coal and other essential industrial goods from Nottinghamshire and Derbyshire. This even included gunpowder, for when the miner required a heavy hand.

Much of the canal is now derelict, with what remains of the route being used for leisurely strolls by the locals. There is an animated waterfront in the city centre that is encircled by bars, public houses, restaurants, and luxury apartments. The Canal Bars comes highly recommended for a cheeky summer tipple. The view from the deck, looking out at the water with the Castle in the distance, is simply unbeatable.

BRITISH
WATERWAYS

14
Lace Market

Nottingham's main luxury trade was in the fine art of lace-making, and was sought after all over the country. In the main hub of The Market the buildings were designed so that sale and promotion could happen on the ground floor shops, with extravagant displays of fashion and furniture whilst housing the factory equipment away from the public view. The Adams Building, now part of New College Nottingham, was developed to have luxuries for the workers such as libraries, a school room, a tea room and a chapel. The area now connects to Hockley forming the 'Creative Quarter' of Nottingham where independent artists and entrepreneurs are encouraged to set up business. If you want to explore the best and kookiest of Nottingham's independent bars, restaurants, and entertainment this is the place to be.

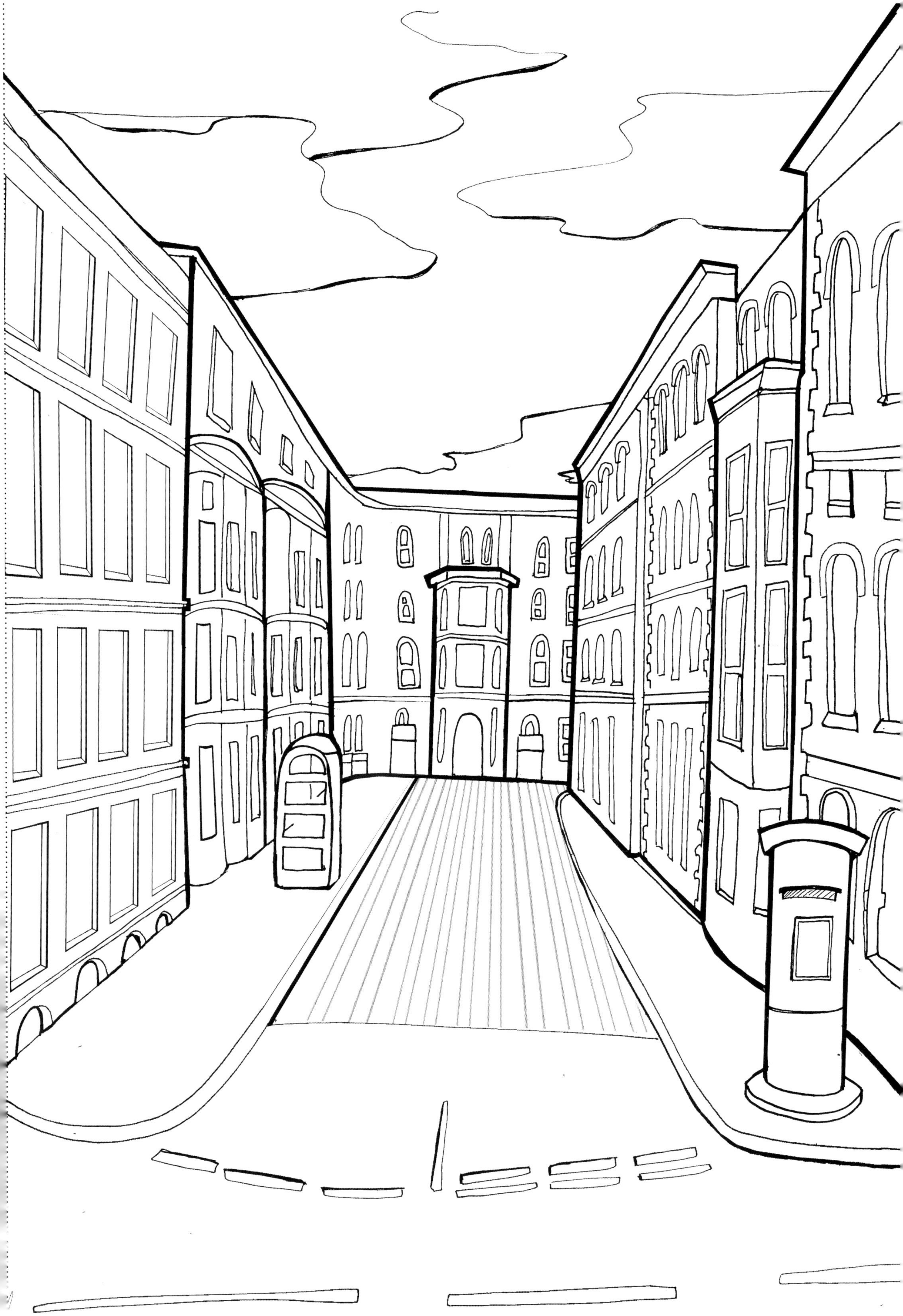

15

Share your colouring! send pictures to @lissieart on facebook!

Newstead Abbey

Most famous for being home to romantic poet Lord Byron, Newstead began as a humble Augustinian Priory (a home and place of worship for Augustine Monks). The Newstead Abbey Estate and Gardens cover 300 acres of land with stunning water features and formal gardens and that's before you enter the house itself.

Lord Byron, was an eccentric, to put it mildly and made some unusual adjustments during his tenor as Lord. The oldest part – the Great Hall - would have been used to host important guests. Lord Byron, had different ideas as to how the space could be used and converted it into a shooting range.

Today the Abbey is managed by Nottingham City Council. It is certainly off the beaten track but worth a visit if you're feeling particularly intrepid.

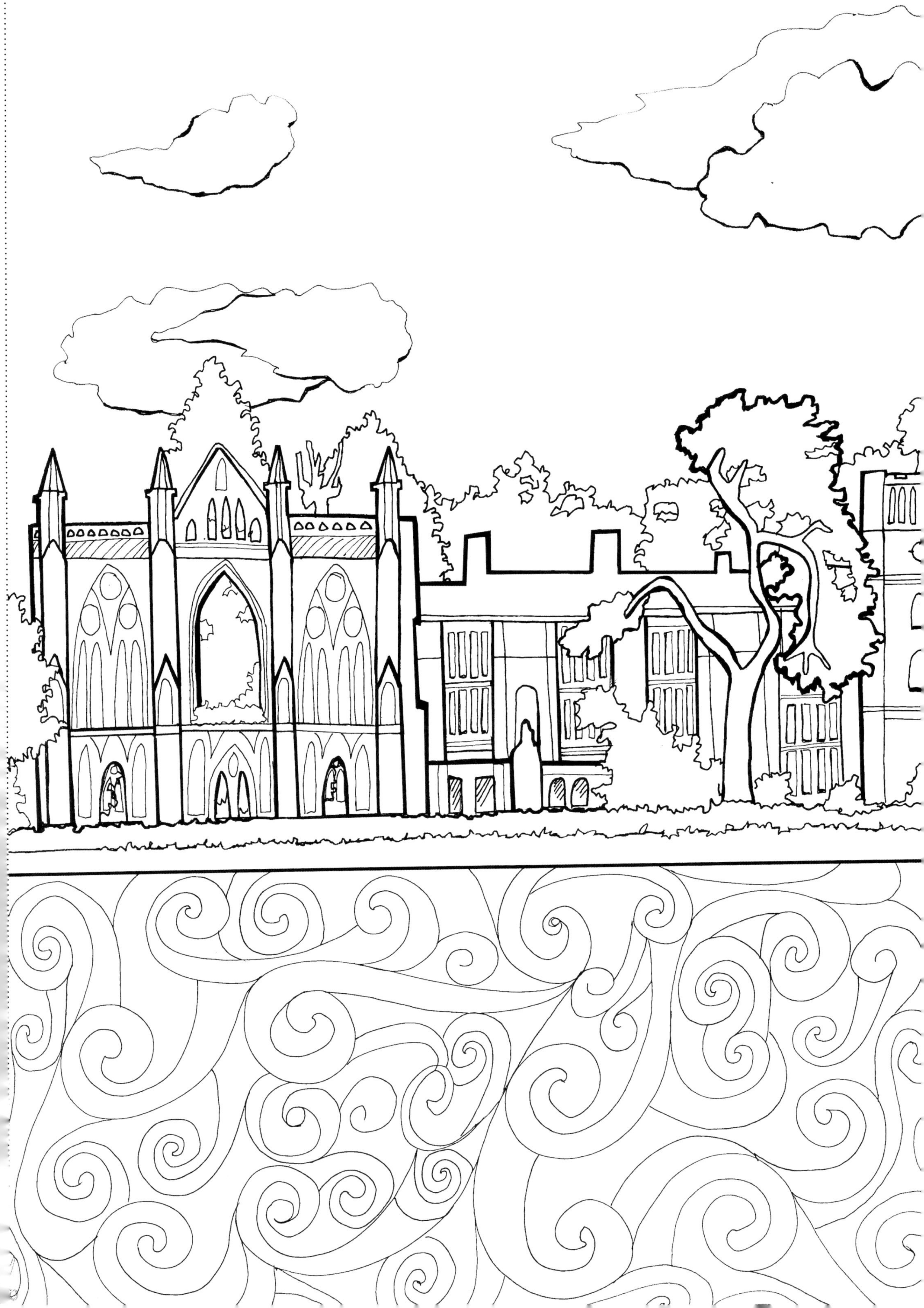

16

TRENT BRIDGE
+THE RIVER TRENT

The most important settlements often spring up around important rivers, and Nottingham is no exception. The River Trent runs through Nottingham and (if you look at the map) flows past Lincolnshire into the North Sea.

In Nottingham, the river splits the two football stadiums for Nottingham Forest and Nottingham City: this fierce rivalry is bridged, appropriately by the Trent Bridge. In the past bridges across the Trent haven't been quite as stable as this modern form; wood of former bridges was easily damaged by floods and washed away, carving the city in two.

Thankfully, engineering has improved immensely since 1551 when the Royal Charter for the Bridge Estate was set up, so we can rest assured that the modern iron and stone construction will stand the test of time.

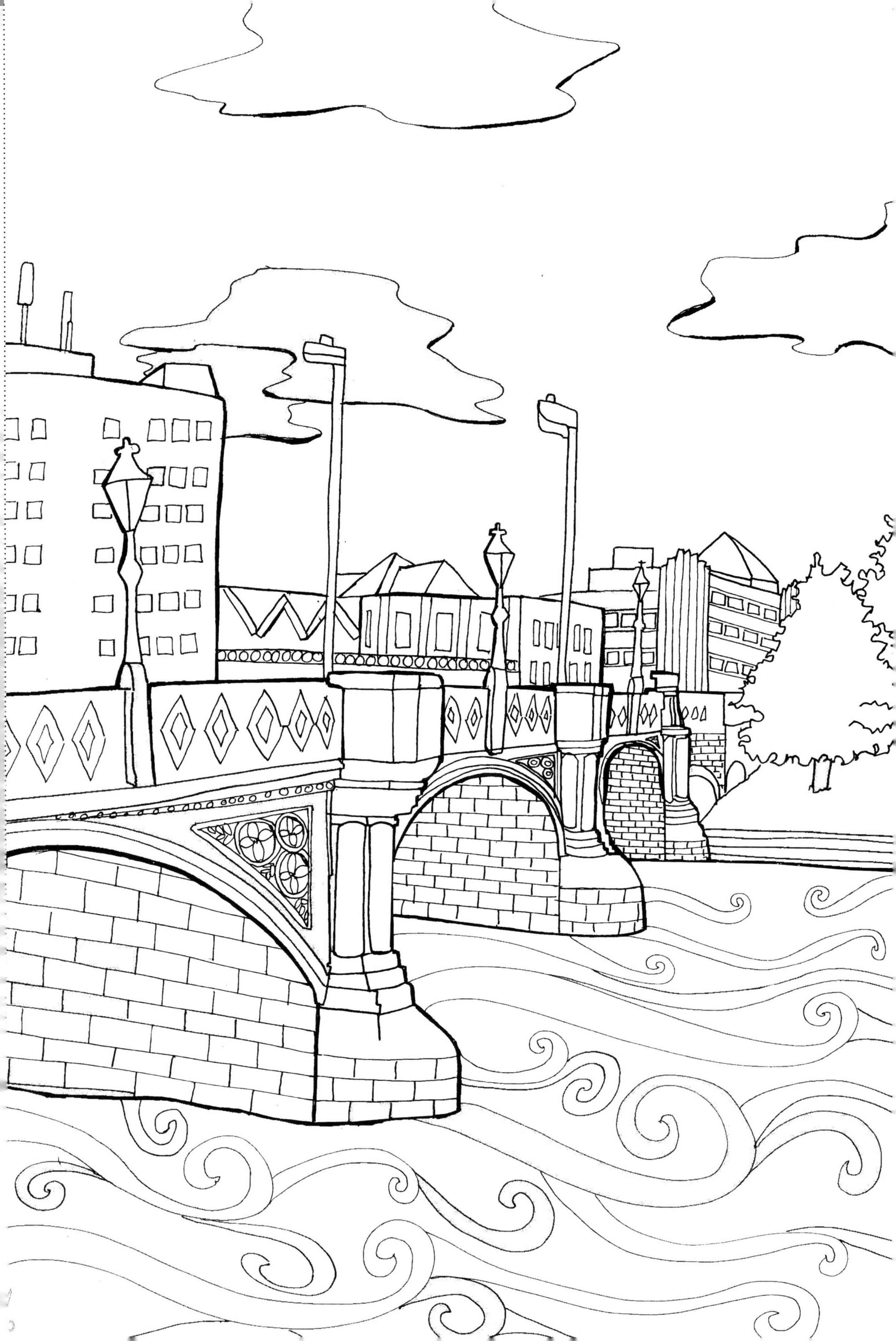

17

THE DUKE OF NEWCASTLE'S TUNNEL
+ THE PARK ESTATE

Located in The Park Estate Nottingham, the tunnel allowed horse drawn carriages to access The Park Estate from Derby Road. Nottingham has plenty of hidden gems, in terms of shops and restaurants, but this is a little nook you can see, no expense required. The steep drop from Newcastle Drive (just off of Derby Road) is both intimidating and quite awe-inspiring. The Park Estate used to be private hunting ground for the Duke of Newcastle who occupied what used to be Nottingham Castle Mansion. It Is now one of the most illustrious addresses in the city, and it's easy to see why.

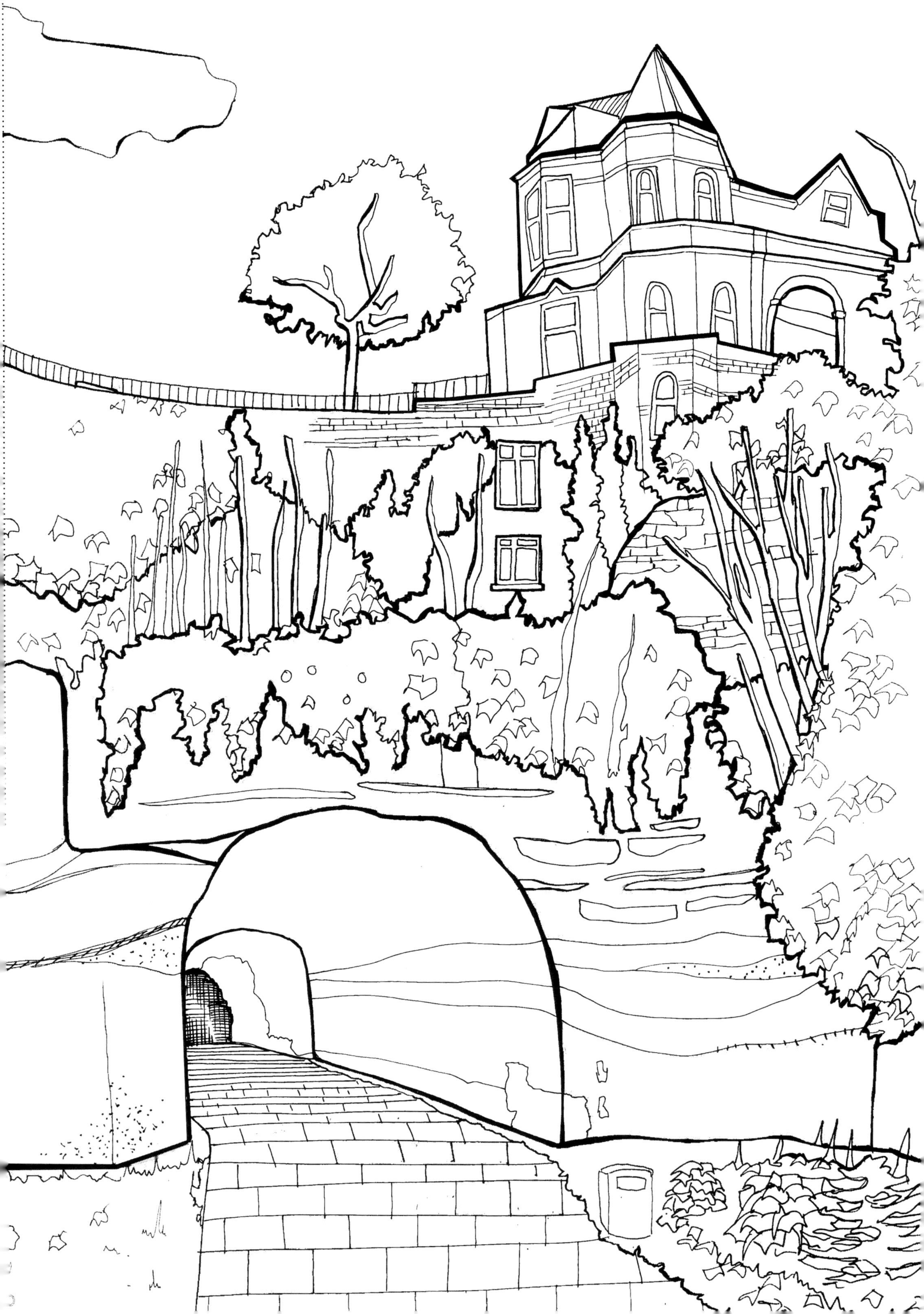

18

YE OLDE TRIP TO JERUSALEM

'The Oldest Pub in England!' Is the claim *Ye Olde Trip to Jerusalem* makes, tracing its history back to 1189. The pub certainly has an air of history about it, with areas being carved into the sandstone rocks, it takes you back in time but with a better selection of ales and more comfortable accommodations than in the past.

Even though the earliest record of an establishment here is recorded as *'The Pilgrim Inn'* in 1751, it would almost certainly have been used as a watering hole prior to this, having been the brewery for the Castle that sits above. With good grub and a great atmosphere, it is well worth a visit.

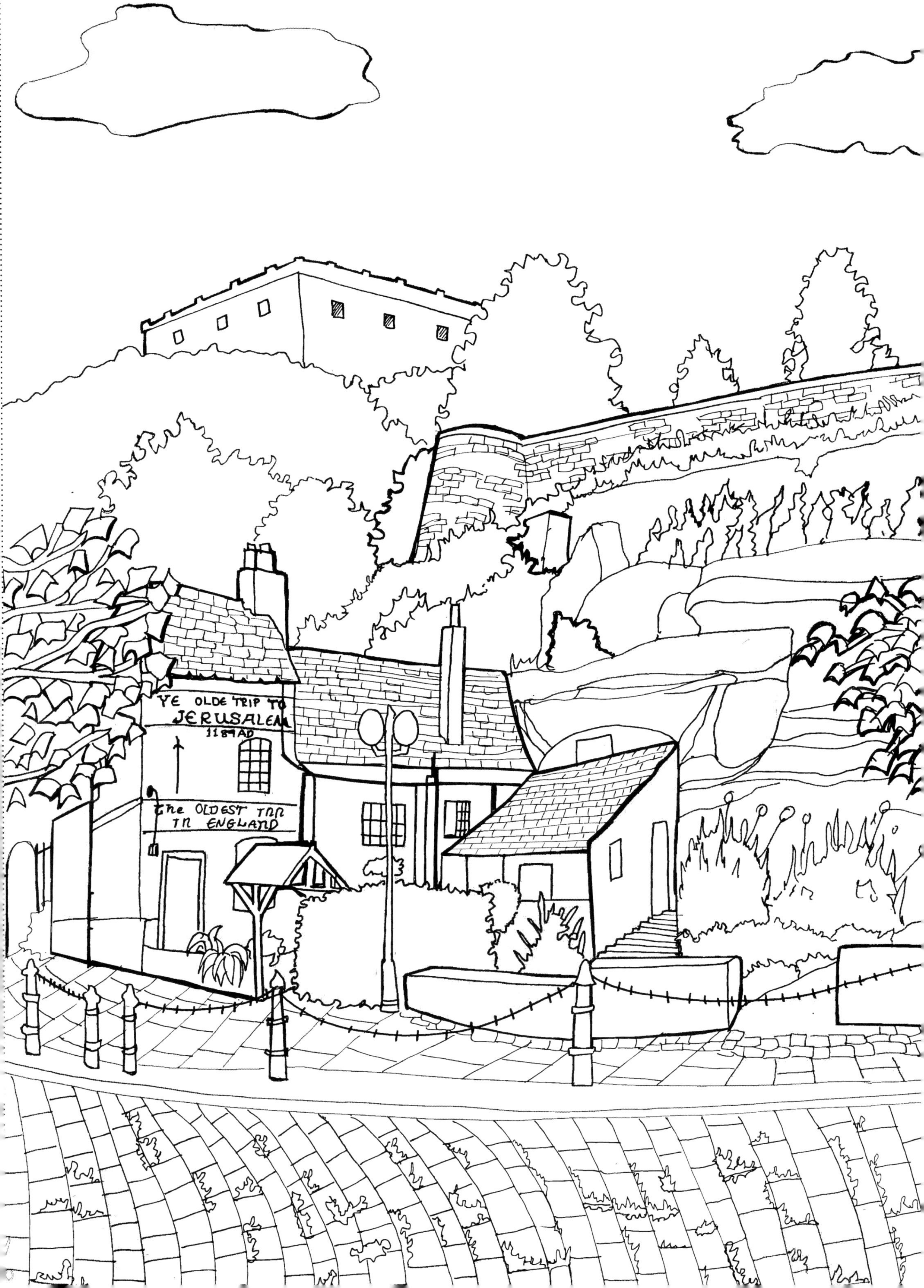
YE OLDE TRIP TO
JERUSALEM
1189AD
The OLDEST INN
IN ENGLAND

19

THE ARBORETUM

The Park is full of beautiful features. It houses over 800 trees on the superbly sustained site. The *tree-trail* is a great place to take a breather; It is a peaceful oasis from the business of the bustling city near-by. It is easily accessed from the tram running nearby, handy considering that it is the site for many community events. Close to Nottingham Trent University housing, students can indulge in the pleasurable views the Arboretum has to offer.

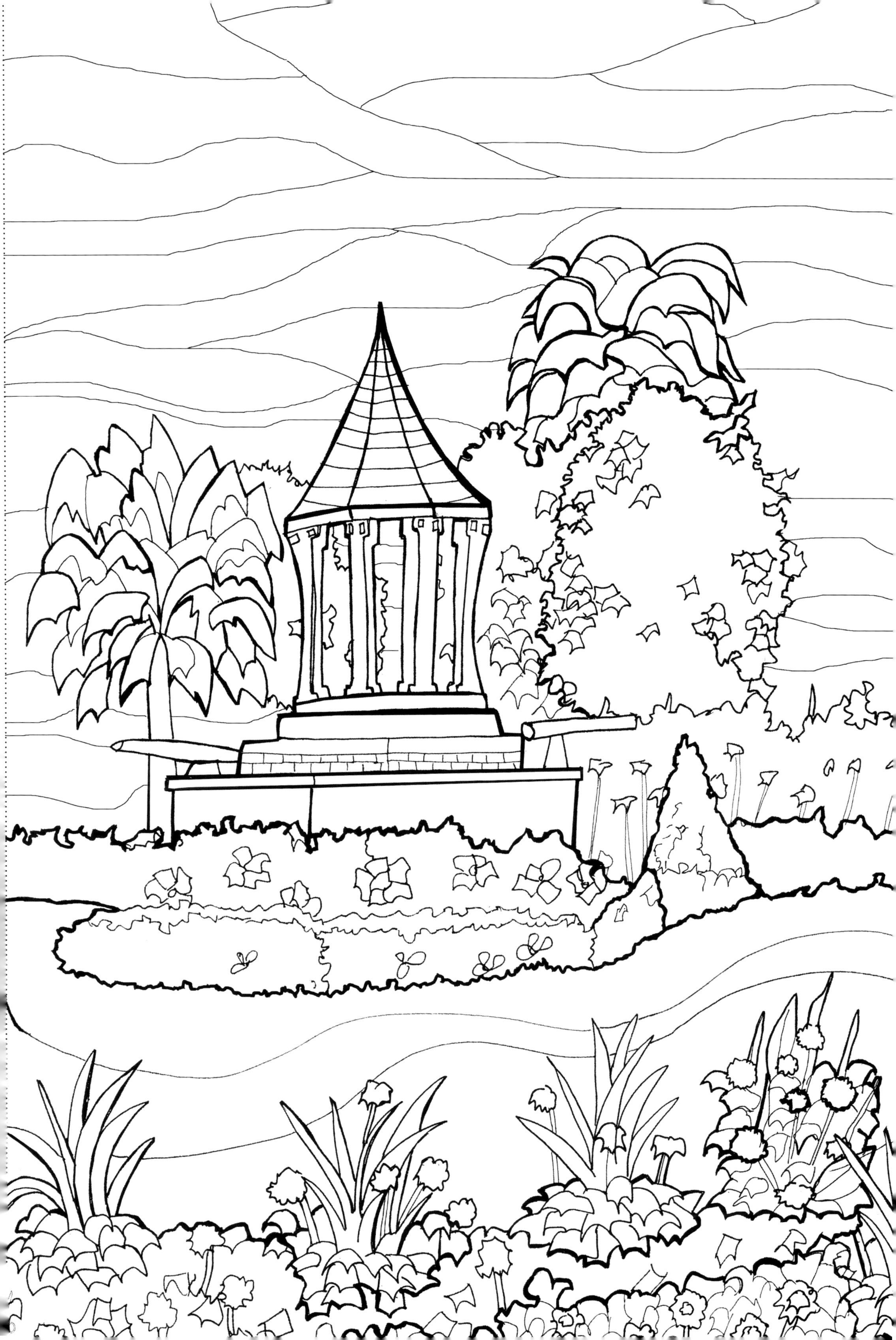

20

Victoria Memorial

The most prominent War Memorial to commemorate Nottingham's fallen is registered as part of the Ancient Monuments Act. The Grade II Listed memorial was opened to the public on Remembrance Day 1927. The site was generously donated by Sir Jesse Boot, founder of the nationwide chemists chain.

The Victoria Embankment, a public area along the River Trent, with 10 miles of concrete steps, is used as part of the annual Riverside Festival which features live music, theatre, spaces for children, fireworks and a Dragon Boat Race that local groups can enter for charity or for fun.

Share your colouring! tag @finelinesbylissie to show the community

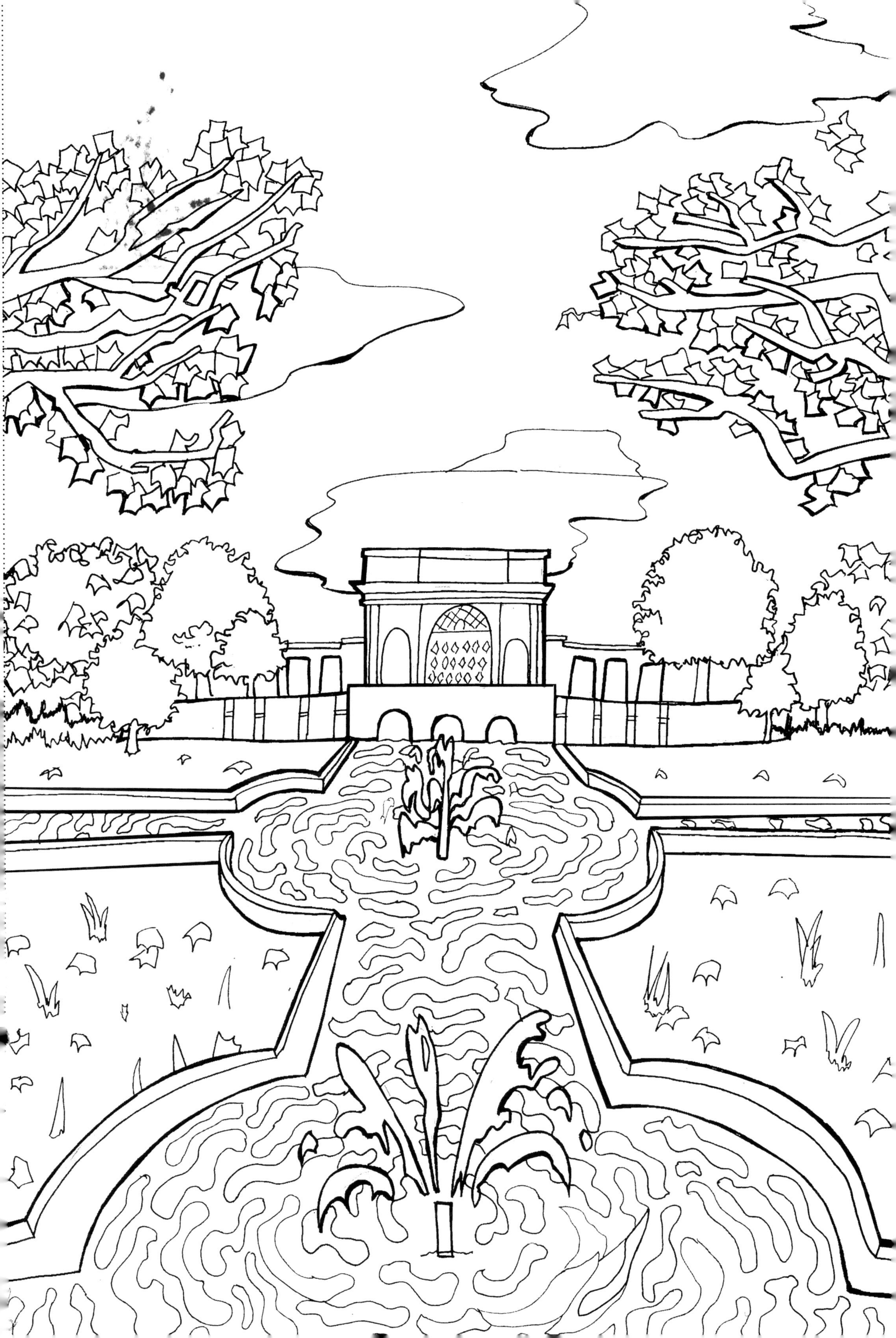

44

For more, check out our social media and website!

www.lissieart.com/finelines

@ finelinesbylissie

Lissieart

FREE EXTRA PAGES AND CUT OUTS!

Go to www.lissieart.com to access exclusive extras

(it's a secret club only for finelines customers... sssshh)

password: ayupmeduck

45

WANT TO GO **BIG?**

Large Prints are available at

www.lissieart.com

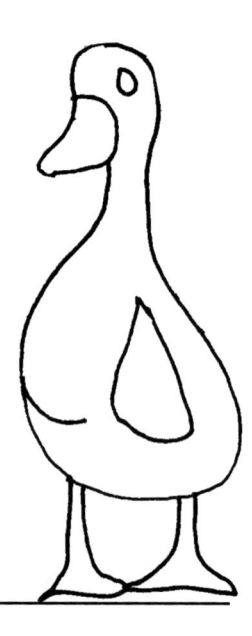

Quack!